# COMPREHENSION SKILLS

# CONCLUSION

## LEVEL F

*Linda Ward Beech*

*Tara McCarthy*

*Donna Townsend*

## STECK-VAUGHN
ELEMENTARY · SECONDARY · ADULT · LIBRARY

A Harcourt Company

www.steck-vaughn.com

| | |
|---|---|
| *Editorial Director:* | Diane Schnell |
| *Project Editor:* | Anne Souby |
| *Associate Director of Design:* | Cynthia Ellis |
| *Design Manager:* | Cynthia Hannon |
| *Media Researcher:* | Christina Berry |
| *Production:* | Rusty Kay |
| *Cover Illustration:* | Stephanie Carter |
| *Cover Production:* | Alan Klemp |
| *Photograph:* | Jack Demuth |

ISBN 0-7398-2656-5

5 6 7 8 9 0  BNG  04 03

Drawing a conclusion means playing detective. You must put all the clues together in order to find the answer.

Look at the picture. The woman in the picture is working. What is her job? Suppose you knew that people with her job have to wear special clothing. Would that change your conclusion? Which parts of the picture give you clues about what she is doing?

# What Is a Conclusion?

A conclusion is a decision you make after thinking about all the information you have. The writer may not state his or her conclusions in a story. As you read, you often have to hunt for clues. These help you understand the whole story. By putting all the clues together, you can draw a conclusion about the information.

There are many stories in this book. You will draw conclusions based on each story you read.

## Try It!

Read this story about tornadoes. Think about the information it gives you.

◆

A tornado is a huge, powerful storm. Because of its shape, the rapidly spinning cloud is sometimes called a funnel cloud. It whirls and spins in the sky and sometimes touches down on the ground. One tornado drove a piece of straw through the trunk of a tree!

What conclusion can you draw about tornadoes? Write your conclusion on the lines below.

_____

_____

You might have written something such as "Tornadoes can cause much destruction" or "Tornadoes can be very dangerous." You can draw these conclusions from the story. The first sentence says that a tornado is a very powerful storm. This conclusion is supported by the example in the last sentence. The third sentence tells you that these dangerous storms sometimes touch the ground. From these clues you can draw the conclusions above.

# Using What You Know

Read each story on this page. Hunt for clues that will help you draw a conclusion about the location of the person telling each story.

I'm wearing a new suit. My hair is nicely combed. I got lost on my way here, but I drove around until I found it. I tucked a few papers into my briefcase. I took a few deep breaths, put on my best smile, and opened the office door. I really hope to get this job.

Where am I? _____

The first thing I do is drop some coins into a slot. Then I hold and point a hose at the car. The water comes out in a powerful spray, so I have to be careful not to put my hand in it. I can choose from cycles such as soap, rinse, and wax.

Where am I? _____

A few cars zoom by. Then a noisy bus passes. If only the light would hurry up and change. I must return the books before the library closes.

Where am I? _____

All I can hear is the wind. There isn't any traffic here. The air is very thin at this altitude. I try to take deep breaths. I think I'll have a snack before I climb any higher. I'm near the top, and I can see down into the valley. But I won't make it to the peak before lunchtime.

Where am I? _____

**To check your answers, turn to page 60.**

# Practice Drawing Conclusions

This book asks you to draw conclusions from the information, or clues, in the stories. Read the example that follows.

◆

> Many flowers produce lovely scents. Butterflies fly to flowers in order to sip the fragrant nectar. You would think that the world's largest flower, the three-foot-wide *monster flower*, would make the air smell nice for miles around. Instead, it smells like rotting garbage. Flies buzz around the giant plant all day long.

 **1.** From the story you can conclude that
    **A.** flies probably drink monster-flower nectar
    **B.** butterflies sometimes smell like rotting garbage
    **C.** most people plant monster flowers in gardens
    **D.** the monster flower was discovered in 1935

The correct answer is **A**. The story says that butterflies fly to flowers in order to sip the fragrant nectar. It also says that flies buzz around the giant plant all day long. Because butterflies sip nectar from the sweet-smelling plants, you can conclude that flies might drink a bad-smelling nectar from the monster flower.

Sometimes a question asks about something you *cannot* tell from a story. Read the example that follows.

◆

> Summers are long and hot in places where the Mississippi River flows into the sea. But people working in the fields found a way to make the days pass more quickly. They sang songs called hollers. Near the turn of the century, people began singing hollers and playing guitars. That's the way in which the type of music called the blues got started.

_____ **2.** From the story you <u>cannot</u> tell
    **A.** where the blues began
    **B.** how jazz was born
    **C.** when the blues began
    **D.** where summers are long and hot

**To check your answer, turn to page 60.**

# How to Use This Book

This book has 25 units with 5 stories in each unit. After you read each story, choose the correct conclusion.

When you finish reading and answering the questions, check your answers by looking at pages 61 and 62. Tear out the answer pages and fold them to the unit you are checking. Write the number of correct answers in the score box at the top of the unit page.

## *Hints for Better Reading*

◆ Read the question carefully. Each question is different. Does the question use the word *not* or the contraction *n't?*

◆ Sometimes the clue to the correct answer lies in the middle of the story. As you look for the answer, read the whole story again.

◆ Read all the answers before choosing the correct one. Sometimes there seems to be more than one correct answer. But only one of them really fits the clues in the story.

## *Challenge Yourself*

Try this special challenge. Read the stories and answer the questions. At least one of the answers is a conclusion that you can draw from the story. Write another conclusion that you can draw from the story.

## *Writing*

On pages 30–31 and 58–59, there are stories with questions. These do not have answers for you to choose. Think of an answer and write it in your own words. You will find suggested answers on page 60, but your answers may be different.

**1.** A gorilla named Koko learned sign language. One day Koko pulled two fingers across her cheeks to indicate whiskers. She wanted a kitten. So she was given one, and she named it All Ball. Koko cuddled and stroked All Ball just as a mother gorilla would stroke a baby gorilla. She dressed All Ball in linen napkins and hats. They also tickled each other. How did Koko feel about All Ball? "Soft, good cat cat," she said in sign language.

**2.** Thomas Jefferson's home, Monticello, is famous. But too many people visited the President there. Jefferson could not turn guests away. So he had another home near Lynchburg, Virginia. It was called Poplar Forest, and Jefferson went there when Monticello got too crowded.

**3.** The *abacus* is an ancient device made of beads that slide on sticks. It is widely thought that the abacus was used by storekeepers and money changers only in Asia. In fact, the abacus was also used in ancient Rome and Greece. The Russian scientists who launched the spacecraft *Sputnik* also used an abacus to do their calculations.

**4.** In the 1800s two brothers were traveling west in a covered wagon. They grew to detest each other so much that one brother sawed the wagon in half and drove away. He left his brother stranded on the prairie with the back half of the wagon and one set of oxen.

**5.** Doug Seuss trains bears to wreck cabins and chase actors in the movies. But the animal trainer believes that the beasts are affectionate and smart. He romps in the creek with his thirteen-hundred-pound friend, Bart. Bart rides in the back of Doug's pickup truck to the car wash. That's where Bart takes a bath.

_____ **1.** From the story you can tell that
   **A.** kittens like to wear hats
   **B.** Koko hates to tickle animals
   **C.** gorillas can be loving and intelligent
   **D.** baby gorillas have whiskers

_____ **2.** For Jefferson, Poplar Forest was a place
   **A.** to get away from the heat at Monticello
   **B.** where he could be a real farmer
   **C.** he liked better than Monticello
   **D.** to be alone

_____ **3.** From the story you can tell that an abacus
   **A.** is used to print money
   **B.** is used to do math
   **C.** is an invention of the Greeks
   **D.** is no longer used today

_____ **4.** The stranded brother probably
   **A.** was angry
   **B.** bought a car
   **C.** read some books
   **D.** was sleepy

_____ **5.** From the story you can tell that
   **A.** bears don't take baths often
   **B.** Bart doesn't like pickups
   **C.** Doug is probably a good animal trainer
   **D.** Bart weighs less than Doug

**1.** The male bowerbird of Australia courts his mate inside a colorful bower, or playhouse. First the bird builds a kind of castle made of towers, huts, and pathways. He decorates this den with butterfly wings, flowers, shells, and stones. Then he waits for the female bowerbird to admire his work.

**2.** The American tarantula is a large, hairy spider. It scares most people when they see it. Fortunately, the spider's bite is harmless. But it can be painful.

**3.** In 1791 surgeon George Hamilton went down with a ship off the coast of Australia. Years later when divers examined the wreck, they found the doctor's silver pocket watch stopped at twelve minutes past eleven. They also found a small bottle with an oily liquid in it. It contained oil of cloves used by the doctor. The liquid was still fragrant after almost two hundred years in the ocean.

**4.** Weather experts can predict rain, snow, and sunshine fairly well. Now scientists can predict where lightning will strike. They can warn airplane pilots to change their routes. Also, people in charge of golf tournaments can adjust the playing schedule.

**5.** The planet Saturn is famous for the rings around it. The rings are made of tiny pieces of matter floating around the planet. The space ship *Voyager 2* has shown that gravity pulls the pieces away from the ring. They fall toward Saturn. As more pieces fall, there appears to be less of a ring.

_____ **1.** You can tell that the male bowerbird
    **A.** cannot fly very far
    **B.** builds its bower to keep out the rain and heat
    **C.** is a coastal bird that eats fish
    **D.** builds its bower to attract a mate

_____ **2.** From this story you can tell that
    **A.** tarantulas move fast
    **B.** all people are afraid of tarantulas
    **C.** tarantulas sting many people
    **D.** most people try to avoid tarantulas

_____ **3.** From the story you can conclude that
    **A.** glass helps preserve liquids under water
    **B.** surgeon Hamilton had many children
    **C.** the divers found the wreck at 11:12 P.M.
    **D.** small bottles hold liquids better than big bottles

_____ **4.** From this story you can tell that
    **A.** experts can predict when lightning will strike
    **B.** airplanes aren't affected by lightning
    **C.** experts are usually in charge of tournaments
    **D.** lightning is a common danger at golf tournaments

_____ **5.** This story suggests that
    **A.** Saturn may not always have its rings
    **B.** Saturn is the only planet to have rings
    **C.** *Voyager 2* changed the rings of Saturn
    **D.** gravity keeps the rings in place

**1.** There's a mouse club in England. The club members judge the mice on qualities such as length of the body, length of the tail, shape of the ears, and brightness of the eyes. The show career for mice is 10 to 12 months, and the background of each mouse is recorded much like that of a racehorse.

**2.** One day two disc jockeys were talking about how fast a driver can go before getting a ticket. The next day one of the disc jockeys said there was a police officer giving tickets on a particular street. The other DJ wanted to know how the first one knew this. The first one said, "Believe me. They give tickets if you go 62 miles per hour."

**3.** A gland about the size of a pea controls how tall or short you are. But too much of this gland's growth fluid causes the bones to grow very long and large. The tallest person measured grew to be 8 feet 11 inches tall and weighed 490 pounds.

**4.** A baseball batter has less than one tenth of a second to decide what type of pitch is coming. Then the brain has to figure out whether or not to swing. The brain also has to tell the batter's muscles what to do to hit the ball.

**5.** One scientist thinks studying should be an "active process." He thinks that making fun of a book that you're reading helps you remember it later. Don't study in the bedroom, the kitchen, or near a TV. You'll wind up sleeping, eating, or watching TV. Instead, go to a library or some other place that will help you think.

_____ **1.** These mice probably
    **A.** have ears shaped like cauliflowers
    **B.** live for five years
    **C.** are judges
    **D.** have papers showing their backgrounds

_____ **2.** From this story you might conclude that
    **A.** the disc jockeys like their work
    **B.** all drivers get speeding tickets
    **C.** the first disc jockey got a ticket
    **D.** police officers like to give tickets

_____ **3.** Too little growth fluid might
    **A.** make people very beautiful
    **B.** cause bones to be shorter than usual
    **C.** cause people to grow big muscles
    **D.** make the hands grow big

_____ **4.** You might conclude that a baseball player
    **A.** must be able to think fast
    **B.** has ten seconds to decide about a pitch
    **C.** must have muscles that think
    **D.** always pitches very quickly

_____ **5.** To study actively you should
    **A.** read the material
    **B.** make a snack and eat it in your bedroom
    **C.** memorize lists
    **D.** talk back to the book

**1.** In 1893 two sisters named Mildred and Patty Hill taught music in a school in Kentucky. They wrote a song for their pupils called "Good Morning to You." Later one of the sisters decided to change two words in the song. "Happy Birthday to You" is now sung and played more than any other song in the world. The melody and the rest of the words are the same as those in the original song.

**2.** The shrew is the smallest mammal in the world. It is about two and one-half inches long. It weighs as much as a dime. To stay alive a shrew must eat its own weight in food every day. If the same were true for human beings, they would have to spend their entire day eating.

**3.** Through time people have paid taxes for many reasons. In ancient Rome people had to pay a tax when they married. Long ago in England, tax bills were sent to men who were not married. There was even a law in Russia that taxed men with beards. At one time in Ireland, people had to pay a tax for the windows in their houses.

**4.** An Egyptian prince named Amun is buried in the United States. His remains lie in a graveyard in Middlebury, Vermont. The baby prince died more than three thousand years before Columbus discovered America. In 1886 the director of a Vermont museum bought the mummy of the prince. Several years later the museum decided to give the little prince a final resting place. The headstone on the grave indicates that Amun was the son of an Egyptian king and queen.

**5.** Each year the Winter Carnival is celebrated in St. Paul, Minnesota. But there hasn't been a carnival as great as the one held in 1866. During that year an ice palace that measured 14 stories high was built. It was made up of 55,000 blocks of ice. It was the site of a wedding attended by more than 6,000 guests. There was even enough room for all of them!

_____ **1.** The sisters' song became popular after
          **A.** their pupils sang it at school
          **B.** they made a change in the words
          **C.** they sang it at a birthday party
          **D.** the tune was changed

_____ **2.** You can conclude that a shrew is always
          **A.** difficult to catch
          **B.** running from enemies
          **C.** looking for food
          **D.** trying to grow

_____ **3.** The story tells you that
          **A.** people have never liked paying taxes
          **B.** people used to pay more taxes than they do now
          **C.** tax laws have always been unfair
          **D.** there have been some unusual taxes

_____ **4.** You can tell that the little prince
          **A.** was buried once before in Egypt
          **B.** was given a very large funeral
          **C.** was buried with gold and jewels
          **D.** was ten years old when he died

_____ **5.** In 1866 the carnival was special because
          **A.** the ice palace was built
          **B.** many people got married
          **C.** it was very cold in St. Paul that year
          **D.** all the snow melted in the spring

**1.** In Tarzan movies, quicksand pulls victims down to their certain deaths. Actually, quicksand does not suck people into it at all. In fact, it is impossible for a person to sink all the way down in quicksand. But people can drown after losing their balance.

**2.** There is a strange boat race every year in Australia's Todd River. A pair of racers stands inside a boat without a bottom. Holding the boat by its sides, they run down the riverbed. The race was cancelled one year when an unusual amount of rain actually filled the Todd River with water.

**3.** Pete Gray wanted to play baseball even though he had lost his right arm at the age of six. He began playing professional baseball in 1943. Two years later he was playing center field with the St. Louis Browns. He batted well, stole bases regularly, and was a good fielder.

**4.** There is actually a summer camp for dogs in New York. The counselors hold treasure hunts for dogs by hiding dog biscuits. The camp sends regular reports about the dogs to their owners. Each report is signed with the dog's paw print.

**5.** One difference between an alligator and a crocodile is that the alligator has a much larger snout. Also, the alligator has an *overbite*. This means that the teeth in its lower jaw fit behind the teeth in its upper jaw. But the bottom and top teeth of the crocodile fit between each other, forming a single row when closed.

_____ **1.** You can tell from this story that
      **A.** people can swim in quicksand
      **B.** quicksand is accurately shown in movies
      **C.** movies exaggerate the danger of quicksand
      **D.** if you fall into quicksand, you can never get out

_____ **2.** From this story you know that
      **A.** the water of the river will hold up a bottomless boat
      **B.** Australia always has plenty of rain
      **C.** the Todd River is usually dry
      **D.** the race will become part of the Summer Olympics

_____ **3.** From the story you can tell that Gray
      **A.** was determined to play baseball
      **B.** played professional baseball more than three years
      **C.** lost his arm while on the job
      **D.** played professional baseball longer than anybody

_____ **4.** You can conclude that the dogs probably
      **A.** learn weaving and crafts on rainy days
      **B.** get homesick often
      **C.** are owned by people who treat their dogs like children
      **D.** are taught tricks by the counselors

_____ **5.** To tell a crocodile from an alligator, you would
      **A.** look at their tails
      **B.** feel their tails
      **C.** look at their eyes
      **D.** look at their mouths

**1.** Only one President has been stopped for speeding while holding office. A police officer stopped Ulysses S. Grant when he was driving a horse and buggy too fast. This was not even Grant's first offense. He was fined five dollars twice before for breaking the speed limit.

**2.** Tomatoes used to be considered poisonous, perhaps because of their bright color. In 1820 a man in Salem, New Jersey, proved that they weren't harmful. Robert Johnson ate an entire basket of tomatoes in front of the whole town. His doctor was there and was sure that Johnson would die.

**3.** Many people believe that margarine was invented during World War II. This substitute for butter was actually made by the French in 1869. It wasn't used widely in the United States because dairy farmers were against its sale. Wisconsin had the last law against it. That law ended in 1967.

**4.** The W was called a hook thousands of years ago. At that time it was shaped like the letter Y. The Romans drew the W like the letter V. Some people in the Middle Ages drew the W as two V's side by side. Other people at that time drew the letter as UU.

**5.** Mechanical clocks are about seven hundred years old. But daily time was measured as many as three thousand years ago. The ancient Egyptians measured time with a shadow stick. It cast a shadow across markers as the sun moved. Another "clock" was a candle marked with numbers.

_____ **1.** From the story you can tell that
  **A.** Grant was stopped for speeding five times
  **B.** speed limits were in use before cars were invented
  **C.** Grant had a special reason for speeding
  **D.** the speed limit was five miles per hour then

_____ **2.** From the story you can tell that
  **A.** some brightly colored plants are poisonous
  **B.** tomatoes are usually dull-looking
  **C.** Johnson was afraid he would die
  **D.** Johnson's doctor liked tomatoes

_____ **3.** You can tell from the story that
  **A.** dairy farmers approved of the use of margarine
  **B.** Wisconsin probably had many dairy farmers
  **C.** French dairy farmers opposed the use of margarine
  **D.** margarine was widely used in America before 1967

_____ **4.** The letter W got its name because it once
  **A.** looked like the letter V
  **B.** was used by the Romans
  **C.** was written UU
  **D.** was called a hook

_____ **5.** You can tell from the story that
  **A.** you can use a shadow stick at night
  **B.** the Egyptians were interested in mechanical clocks
  **C.** measuring time has interested people for ages
  **D.** people have always measured time with candles

**1.** Don't let people ever tell you that they caught a sardine with a fishing pole. *Sardine* doesn't refer to any particular fish. It is used to describe any small fish that can be canned. Young herring are often used as sardines.

**2.** The words of the song "The Star-Spangled Banner" were written by Francis Scott Key. He wrote the words in 1812 during a war that America fought against the British. But the tune is not original. It was taken from a British song popular at the time.

**3.** A New Yorker invented something called a scootboard. It is like the scooters that people stand on and push with one foot. But the scootboard has a bicycle wheel in front. It also has an engine. The person stands on the narrow platform and uses hand controls. The scootboard can travel thirty miles per hour.

**4.** The stories of wolves attacking and eating human beings are false. There isn't any record of a wolf attacking a human being in the United States. Only a wolf with rabies would bite a human being. Rabies is a disease that strikes dogs and foxes as well.

**5.** Over time some words in the English language have changed meaning. *Liquor* once meant "any kind of liquid, even water." The word *meat* once meant "any kind of food." In the fourteenth century, *girl* meant "either a young man or woman."

_____ **1.** From the story you know that
    **A.** sardines are actually young herring
    **B.** sardines like to go fishing
    **C.** *sardine* doesn't refer to a canned fish
    **D.** a person might find young herring in a sardine can

_____ **2.** America's national song is interesting because
    **A.** Francis Scott Key didn't write it
    **B.** it was written during a war
    **C.** it was taken from America's enemy at the time
    **D.** it is difficult for most people to sing

_____ **3.** Scootboards may <u>not</u> be popular because
    **A.** hand controls direct the engine
    **B.** they may not be safe
    **C.** they can go thirty miles per hour
    **D.** most scootboard owners are children

_____ **4.** From the story you can tell that
    **A.** wolves are dangerous to human beings
    **B.** there is only one case of a wolf attack on a human
    **C.** there are few wolves in North America
    **D.** wolves are no more dangerous than dogs

_____ **5.** The older meanings of these words were
    **A.** narrower than today's meanings
    **B.** broader than today's meanings
    **C.** not related to today's meanings
    **D.** changed after the fourteenth century

**1.** The potato has traveled quite a bit. It was first grown by the Inca people of South America. Spanish explorers took the plant back with them to Europe, where it grew well. Later the Europeans settled North America. When they did, they brought potatoes back to this side of the Atlantic Ocean.

**2.** An artist named Kurt Ossenfort produces unusual drawings. They are made by trees. He sets up the easel and canvas next to a tree that he likes. Then he ties a pen to the tip of a branch so that it touches the canvas. The wind blows the pen around. His favorite drawing is one by a white oak.

**3.** In Africa it is common to see women carrying heavy loads on their heads. Scientists are surprised by how little energy these women use. A male army recruit carrying 70 percent of his body weight on his back uses 100 percent more oxygen to do so. A woman carrying 70 percent of her body weight on her head increases her oxygen use by only 50 percent.

**4.** The London Bridge from the nursery song was a stone bridge made in the twelfth century. It had shops and homes built into it. These were always catching on fire or needing repair. The bridge was replaced in the 1800s.

**5.** Almost all cats purr, but they never purr when they're alone. They purr only around other cats or human beings. That makes animal experts think that purring is a form of cat talk. It may be a sign that a cat is willing to submit itself to another cat or a person.

_____ **1.** You can conclude that probably
   **A.** the Inca brought the first potato to the United States
   **B.** the potato is grown only in the mountains
   **C.** the potato did not take a direct route to North America
   **D.** potatoes were first grown in Africa

_____ **2.** From the story you can tell that
   **A.** Kurt Ossenfort is sad
   **B.** the drawings are different from photographs
   **C.** the drawings are all of nearby trees
   **D.** the drawings are just one dot on each canvas

_____ **3.** From the story you can tell that
   **A.** army recruits are weaker than African women
   **B.** scientists are often surprised
   **C.** it is impossible for women to carry heavy loads
   **D.** the head carries loads with less energy than the back

_____ **4.** From the story you can tell
   **A.** whether the people in London liked the bridge
   **B.** why the homes and shops caught fire
   **C.** why the song says, "London Bridge is falling down"
   **D.** why the bridge in the song had shops and homes

_____ **5.** This story suggests that
   **A.** cats purr when they are relaxed
   **B.** cats purr when they are afraid
   **C.** cats always purr when they're alone
   **D.** purring is a form of breathing

**1.** *Acrophobia* means "fear of heights." People who have this fear are known as acrophobics. They aren't any less afraid even when there are fences or railings to protect them.

**2.** Most slaves didn't become famous. But Aesop was unusual. He was a clever, witty Greek slave. He earned his freedom through his cleverness. He used his animal fables for the purpose of teaching people to respect the rights of others. Two thousand years later, people continue to use his stories to teach lessons or gain helpful advice.

**3.** The *akita* is a Japanese hunting dog with short, bristly hair. It is considered a symbol of good health. In fact, the dog is so prized that it has been made an official national treasure. The first akita was brought into this country in 1937. Its owner was Helen Keller, the author who was blind and deaf.

**4.** The *anableps* is a freshwater fish found in Mexico and parts of South America. It is unusual because of its eyes. A band of skin divides each eye in half, giving it four eyes. It stays near the top of the water. It can look above and below the water at the same time.

**5.** Today's typewriter and computer keyboard was designed to slow down the speed of typing. The first typists typed too fast. This made the typewriters jam. The keys were arranged as they are today in order to force the typists to slow down.

_____ **1.** From this story you can tell that
    **A.** acrophobics probably don't work in tall buildings
    **B.** many people suffer from acrophobia
    **C.** fences make acrophobics feel better
    **D.** people can get over acrophobia

_____ **2.** From this story you can tell that
    **A.** some Greeks were slaves
    **B.** the Greek people never freed a slave
    **C.** people have finally learned to respect others
    **D.** many slaves became famous after they were freed

_____ **3.** From this story you can tell that akitas
    **A.** are bred in northern Japan
    **B.** were brought to the United States before 1937
    **C.** are valued for more than their hunting ability
    **D.** became very popular in the United States

_____ **4.** You can conclude that the anableps
    **A.** needs bifocals
    **B.** has extremely sensitive skin
    **C.** can't be caught with a rod and reel
    **D.** hunts for food above and below the water

_____ **5.** From this story you can tell that
    **A.** the arrangement of keys affects the speed of typing
    **B.** the designer did not know much about typing
    **C.** typewriters have always had the same keyboard
    **D.** the arrangement of keys doesn't affect typing speed

**1.** The giant saguaro cactus is often seen in Western movies. Although the largest plants can grow to be fifty feet tall, they grow very slowly at first. The stem of the plant grows about one inch during its first ten years, but later it grows at a faster rate. The largest saguaros can live for almost two hundred years.

**2.** You may have seen movies in which the Roman emperor turns his thumb down to show that a gladiator should die. Actually, the gory Roman custom was to turn a thumb up toward the heart for death. A thumb down meant that the soldier should be allowed to live.

**3.** In New York's Federal Reserve Bank, workers handle money and other valuable metals. One of the heaviest things workers must carry is a gold brick. For this reason, some of them wear special shoes made of magnesium. These shoes protect workers' toes if a brick falls on them.

**4.** Sleepwalking is most common among children 10 to 12 years old. Experts think that it is linked to the growth and development of children. But people who sleepwalk can easily hurt themselves. They may also be so confused that they will try to strike the people who awaken them.

**5.** Elizabeth Tashjian runs a nut museum. The museum is found on the first floor of an old mansion, which is also her home. Her collection of nuts from around the world is always being raided by bushy-tailed thieves that live near the house.

_____ **1.** From the story you can conclude
  **A.** why the cactus grows slowly at first
  **B.** why the cactus is seen in the movies
  **C.** exactly what the cactus looks like
  **D.** that the stem grows at different rates at different times

_____ **2.** You can tell that death probably occurred
  **A.** once out of every five times
  **B.** when the emperor gave a thumbs-down
  **C.** when the emperor gave a thumbs-up
  **D.** only in the movies, and not in real-life Rome

_____ **3.** From this story you can tell that magnesium
  **A.** is a harder metal than gold
  **B.** is a softer metal than gold
  **C.** is a more valuable metal than gold
  **D.** is a more comfortable material than leather

_____ **4.** From this story you know that you should
  **A.** always try to wake someone who is sleepwalking
  **B.** be careful when waking a sleepwalker
  **C.** expect children under eight to sleepwalk
  **D.** not worry about someone who is sleepwalking

_____ **5.** Tashjian doesn't call the police because
  **A.** she doesn't like police officers
  **B.** the thieves are squirrels and chipmunks
  **C.** the police don't take her seriously
  **D.** she feeds the nuts to her horse

**1.** Some animals can help predict earthquakes. This was proved in China in 1974. Just a few months before a huge earthquake struck an area in China, animals began acting strangely. Hens wouldn't roost, and geese wouldn't fly. Pigs tried climbing walls and fought with each other. Even hibernating snakes crawled out of the ground. The Chinese paid attention to these warnings. Many people left the area two days before the earthquake struck.

**2.** Freddie Stowers was a soldier in the United States Army. In 1918 Stowers became one of the heroes of World War I. He led his troops on a charge to take a hill held by the Germans. Stowers was killed during the fight. In 1991 Stowers was honored for his actions. He was awarded the Medal of Honor and became the first African American to win the medal for bravery in World War I.

**3.** Women generally have shorter vocal cords than men. Shorter cords vibrate faster, which makes the pitch of the voice higher. This causes women to have higher voices. Women also need less air to vibrate their vocal cords. So most women are able to talk longer and with less effort than most men.

**4.** In 1910 the mayor of Los Angeles asked Alice Wells to join the police force. She was the first policewoman in the United States. Her trailblazing work helped other women. By 1916 there were policewomen in 26 cities.

**5.** A little luck helps in golf. But some golfers seem to get more than their share of luck. In 1979 a player on an Australian golf course made a hole-in-one on the thirteenth and fourteenth holes! Her name was Sue Press.

_____ **1.** The story suggests that
  **A.** some animals have a sixth sense
  **B.** many earthquakes have occurred in China
  **C.** the pigs were fighting with the chickens
  **D.** animals in China act strange all the time

_____ **2.** From this story you can tell that
  **A.** Stowers is still alive
  **B.** Stowers was a member of the German army
  **C.** Stowers fought in the Civil War
  **D.** his medal was not awarded for many years

_____ **3.** You can conclude that most women
  **A.** talk louder than men
  **B.** have higher voices because their cords vibrate faster
  **C.** talk faster than men
  **D.** talk more than men

_____ **4.** The story suggests that
  **A.** Alice Wells wanted to be mayor
  **B.** the mayor didn't think much of Wells
  **C.** Los Angeles set an example for other cities
  **D.** Wells did nothing unusual

_____ **5.** You can tell from the story that
  **A.** Sue Press loved playing golf
  **B.** Press was learning how to golf
  **C.** Press didn't score a hole-in-one on the twelfth hole
  **D.** Press often had bad luck

**1.** Many people take aspirin for aches and pains. Aspirin was first sold around 1900 by the Bayer Company of Germany. It was sold under the trademark Aspirin. Then World War I swept across the world, and Germany lost the war. Under its terms of surrender, Germany agreed to release the trademark. The name Aspirin could no longer be used to sell only Bayer's product. It became the common name of a drug for pain.

**2.** People around the world eat many different things. Some people eat worms and ants. In the Philippines termites are considered a healthy food. They make delicious, bite-sized snacks. Termites are especially tasty when served together with hamburgers.

**3.** Dennis Chávez served in the United States Senate for more than twenty years. He was the first Hispanic to hold the post of senator. He was born in an adobe house in New Mexico. As a boy he learned to speak English and taught it to his family. In 1920 he graduated from law school. Fifteen years later he was elected senator from New Mexico. In 1991 a postage stamp with his picture was issued. The stamp honors his service to the country.

**4.** Do you like peanut butter? Most people do. Naturally, peanut butter is made from peanuts. But peanuts are used in the manufacture of other things. Items such as ink dyes, shaving cream, paper, and shoe polish use peanuts in some form.

**5.** Mary Elizabeth Bowser was born a slave near Richmond, Virginia. When her master, John Van Lew, died, Mrs. Van Lew sent Mary to Philadelphia to get an education. Then the Civil War began. Mary went back to Richmond. She worked as a spy with Mrs. Van Lew. Serving at the Confederate White House, she listened to the dinner conversations of Jefferson Davis. Each night she would tell Mrs. Van Lew all that was said.

_____ **1.** From the story you can tell that
    **A.** Germany did not fight in World War I
    **B.** aspirin was first sold in Greenland
    **C.** an unusual condition of surrender was met
    **D.** aspirin is no longer sold anywhere

_____ **2.** The story suggests that
    **A.** Filipino and American eating habits differ
    **B.** hamburgers are made of ants and worms
    **C.** everyone in the world eats the same things
    **D.** termites are better than worms

_____ **3.** From this story you can tell that Chávez
    **A.** was elected senator from New Jersey
    **B.** is no longer senator from New Mexico
    **C.** never learned to speak English
    **D.** worked at the post office

_____ **4.** The story suggests that
    **A.** peanut butter is a good shaving cream
    **B.** shoe polish tastes like peanut butter
    **C.** it is easy to write on a peanut
    **D.** peanuts are very useful

_____ **5.** You can conclude that
    **A.** John Van Lew was a cruel master
    **B.** Mrs. Van Lew respected Mary Elizabeth Bowser
    **C.** Bowser studied art in Philadelphia
    **D.** Mrs. Van Lew and Bowser were the same age

# Writing

Read each paragraph. Think about a conclusion you can draw. Write your conclusion in a complete sentence.

**1.** Polo is a game played on horseback. Each team has four players who attempt to hit a ball with their sticks. Each player has to handle the stick with his or her right hand and control the horse with the left hand. The team that scores more goals wins. Goals are scored by hitting the ball inside the other team's goalposts.

What conclusion can you draw from this paragraph?

_____

_____

**2.** Phillis Wheatley was born in Africa. At the age of eight, she was brought to America as a slave. There she learned English and Latin, and she managed to gain her freedom. In 1770 she published her first poem. After that she gained fame as a poet. She even shared her poetry with others when she made a trip to England in 1773.

What conclusion can you draw from this paragraph?

_____

_____

**3.** Alonso is building a weather station. He wants to record details about the weather in his town. So far he has a thermometer to measure air temperature, a gauge to measure rainfall, and a windsock to check wind direction. He still needs something to measure snowfall.

What conclusion can you draw from this paragraph?

_____

_____

**To check your answers, turn to page 60.**

Read the paragraph below. What conclusions can you draw? Use the clues in the paragraph to answer the questions in complete sentences.

Juneteenth is a holiday in Texas. It's also celebrated by some people in California and other western states. It can be traced back to the time Union troops arrived in Texas on June 19, 1865. They brought news that the Civil War had ended and that all the slaves were free. This put an end to slavery in Texas. Juneteenth got its name from some people in Texas who had their own way to say "June 19th." And their way stuck!

**1.** Is Juneteenth a holiday in all states? How do you know?

_____

_____

**2.** Was there slavery in Texas? How do you know?

_____

_____

**3.** Before the Union troops arrived, did Texans know the Civil War was over? How do you know?

_____

_____

**4.** Did Californians coin the word *Juneteenth*? How do you know?

_____

_____

**To check your answers, turn to page 60.**

**1.** Man o' War was a wonderful racehorse. He won 20 of 21 races and set 5 world records. When Man o' War died in 1947, his owner Samuel Riddle had him buried. Riddle, who died in 1963, remembered the horse in his last will and testament. He left $4,000,000 to maintain Man o' War's grave.

**2.** In the 1800s miners carried canaries into the mines with them. The canaries not only provided music but also served an important purpose. If the birds stopped singing, it was a signal to the miners that there was little oxygen left in the mine.

**3.** William Pace was a pig farmer in Mississippi. But he didn't raise his pigs in the ordinary way. Instead of letting the pigs wallow in the mud and heat, he fattened the creatures in the barn by using a giant fan and a television set. Pace believed that the pigs were happier if they could watch TV. The pigs' favorite show seemed to be wrestling!

**4.** Sarah Winnemucca worked to protect Native American rights. Her father was a chief of the Paiute tribe in Nevada. As a child she moved to California, where she lived with a white family. She attended school and learned to speak English. As an adult she became a teacher and tried to make peace between the white settlers and her native tribe. She even met to discuss the situation with President Hayes.

**5.** Most people are afraid of something. A study was conducted to determine the things that people fear most. The research found that men and women tend to have the same fears. The basic difference is the order in which they rate these fears. For example, men fear bats and speaking in public the most. Women fear fire, dead people, and rats the most.

_____ **1.** From the story you <u>cannot</u> tell
    **A.** when Man o' War died
    **B.** how many races Man o' War won
    **C.** when Samuel Riddle died
    **D.** where Man o' War is buried

_____ **2.** The story suggests that canaries
    **A.** were good miners
    **B.** needed enough air to sing
    **C.** were useless to the miners
    **D.** needed darkness to sing

_____ **3.** You can conclude that William Pace
    **A.** thought happy pigs grew fatter
    **B.** used regular ways to raise pigs
    **C.** lived in Missouri
    **D.** trained his pigs to wrestle

_____ **4.** From the story you <u>cannot</u> tell
    **A.** where Winnemucca's tribe lived
    **B.** that Winnemucca spoke English
    **C.** the name of Winnemucca's father
    **D.** what Winnemucca did as an adult

_____ **5.** From the story you can tell that
    **A.** male and female fears are alike and yet different
    **B.** everyone likes rats
    **C.** women fear bats more than men do
    **D.** everyone is afraid of chickens

**1.** The Mohawks are native to New York, and they have always shown a special quality. They have no fear of heights and are very nimble. For this reason most of the skyscrapers in New York City were built by Mohawk workers. They came by subway from their settlement in Brooklyn.

**2.** You may have enough to worry about without worrying about meteorites hitting you. But it does happen. The last victim, Mrs. E. H. Hodges, was hit in 1954. An eight-and-a-half-pound space rock went through the roof of her house, bounced off a radio, and struck her. She was bruised but not seriously hurt.

**3.** The song "Old Folks at Home" starts with the line, "Way down upon the Swanee River." Stephen Foster, the song's author, never saw the river. It is actually called the Suwannee and is located in Florida. The name Suwannee was a way of saying the river's original name, the San Juan.

**4.** On Uranus, the seventh planet in our solar system, the seas may be made up of boiling water. The air glows in the dark. The days are just about 17 hours long, and the temperature of the air may be about 400 degrees below freezing.

**5.** Canada has two official languages. All advertising must be in both French and English across the country. Some employees of the federal government must pass a test in both French and English. Children can learn both French and English in school from a very early age.

_____ **1.** From this story you <u>cannot</u> tell
      **A.** where the Mohawk workers lived
      **B.** which special qualities the Mohawks possess
      **C.** why the Mohawks were hired
      **D.** how many Mohawks worked on the skyscrapers

_____ **2.** The danger of meteorites is slight because
      **A.** they are so small
      **B.** Mrs. Hodges was reading a book
      **C.** they seldom fall
      **D.** people spend most of their time indoors

_____ **3.** To be true to history, Foster should have
      **A.** sailed on the river before writing the song
      **B.** written, "Down by the old folks at home"
      **C.** written, "Way down upon the San Juan River"
      **D.** written, "Way down upon the Swanee River"

_____ **4.** You can conclude that it would be necessary to
      **A.** wear special clothing if you were to visit Uranus
      **B.** know why the air glows
      **C.** know how many seas there are on Uranus
      **D.** know that Uranus is in our solar system

_____ **5.** From this story you can tell that
      **A.** most Canadians are French citizens
      **B.** some Canadians speak both French and English
      **C.** many Canadians speak Spanish
      **D.** France is part of Canada

**UNIT 15**

**1.** At one time there were fewer than one hundred trumpeter swans left in the world. The giant birds were hunted for their skin and quills. Their soft feathers were used in making powder puffs. But people began to care for the swans. By 1999 there were about twenty thousand of these graceful birds left.

**2.** July 4 is a very American day. The Declaration of Independence was signed on this day. President Calvin Coolidge was born on July 4. Three Presidents died on this date. John Adams and Thomas Jefferson died in 1826. James Monroe died in 1831. Also, work on the Washington Monument began on July 4, 1848.

**3.** A hurricane is a strong storm with wind spirals and heavy rain. The direction of the spiral is clockwise south of the equator. North of the equator, it spins the opposite way. Hurricanes are known by various names in different parts of the world. In the North Pacific, a hurricane is called a typhoon. In Australia, it's called a willy-willy.

**4.** D-Day took place in June 1944. The Allied troops invaded France. The Germans wanted to find out where the invasion would start. Their spy planes saw a build-up of tanks and jeeps and an oil refinery at one place in England. They reported this. But the vehicles were inflated rubber, and the oil refinery was a fake. It had been put together by movie-set designers. The fakes were not part of the real invasion.

**5.** The name of a city on an island in the Pacific Ocean is written *Pago Pago*. It is pronounced "Pango Pango." The missionaries who came to the island printed the name of the town in Latin. But their sets of type were short of *n*'s, so they left the *n*'s out of the city's name.

◯

_____ **1.** Trumpeter swans are no longer hunted
     **A.** because there are fewer than one hundred left
     **B.** since their skin and quills dried up
     **C.** because people began to care about them
     **D.** because powder puffs are no longer used

_____ **2.** From this story you <u>cannot</u> tell
     **A.** the year of Calvin Coolidge's death
     **B.** the beginning date of the Washington Monument
     **C.** which Presidents died on that day
     **D.** when Calvin Coolidge was born

_____ **3.** From the story you can tell that hurricanes
     **A.** are much like tornadoes
     **B.** occur more often in South America
     **C.** spin counterclockwise in America
     **D.** destroy everything in their paths

_____ **4.** From this story you can tell that the invasion
     **A.** took place in Germany
     **B.** used rubber tanks and jeeps
     **C.** was planned to start from France
     **D.** took the Germans completely by surprise

_____ **5.** You can probably conclude that
     **A.** the missionaries liked the islanders
     **B.** the native language was difficult to learn
     **C.** the missionaries should have left out another letter
     **D.** the missionaries wrote about the area

**1.** Restaurants come in many shapes in Los Angeles, California. One building looks like a large chili bowl. Another one is shaped like a hot dog. For a fast snack, you can drive through a building that looks like two doughnuts.

**2.** Travelers often stop to wonder at unusual buildings. There's a house made of salt in Grand Saline, Texas. Both Kentucky and Tennessee have houses built from coal. In a town in Maine, visitors gape at a building made from paper. A tour of a house in Florida tells how this house was carved from coral.

**3.** One of the deadliest fish in the world is the puffer. In Japan this fish is called fugu. Some people in Japan like to eat fugu. Cooks have been trained to remove the poisonous parts from the fish. Then they arrange the raw fish into beautiful designs and serve it. Even so, as many as fifty Japanese die from fugu poison each year.

**4.** Scientists are working to make computers think more like people. People say things such as "add a little more." Today's computers cannot understand "little." *Little* is not a real amount. They can only understand terms such as *five ounces*.

**5.** Alice Childress wrote *A Hero Ain't Nothin' but a Sandwich*. The novel tells the story of Benjie Johnson. Benjie is a 13-year-old boy. His life becomes difficult when he gets involved with the wrong people.

_____ **1.** You can conclude that
   **A.** these restaurants serve the best food
   **B.** all the restaurants serve doughnuts
   **C.** these buildings were designed by cooks
   **D.** the shapes tell about the main food served

_____ **2.** You can tell that unusual houses are
   **A.** tourist attractions
   **B.** pleasant to live in
   **C.** not very popular
   **D.** usually built of wood

_____ **3.** From this story you can tell that
   **A.** eating fugu is safe
   **B.** most Japanese eat fugu
   **C.** eating fugu is a daring deed
   **D.** puffers are found only in Japan

_____ **4.** From this story you can tell that
   **A.** computers will think like people in twenty years
   **B.** computers would not understand *a bunch*
   **C.** people think like machines
   **D.** computers give the wrong information

_____ **5.** This story does <u>not</u> tell
   **A.** who the author of the book is
   **B.** what the title of the book is
   **C.** how old Benjie is
   **D.** how Benjie solves his problems

**1.** The name John Wayne is often used to describe a perfect soldier or military hero. The actor John Wayne made movies in which he played tough, strong soldiers. But oddly enough, he never actually served in the armed forces.

**2.** Carlo and Magda wanted to do something for Jo. Jo had scored a winning goal in their last game. Carlo and Magda decided to throw a big party. They invited 25 people. They decorated the backyard in a cheerful manner.

**3.** Experts study people who are good at influencing others. They find that people with influence can figure out what other people want and why they want it. They can do this even when the people say they want something else or give reasons that aren't the real ones.

**4.** In the United States, people use the phrase *national holiday* for days such as July 4 and Labor Day. But there aren't any such holidays. The federal government does not have the power to make one day a holiday for the whole country. Each state votes on whether or not to make a certain day a legal holiday.

**5.** Scientists used to think that the praying mantis was deaf. Today they know that the praying mantis has one ear near its stomach. No other creature of any kind is known to have only one ear.

_____ **1.** From this story you <u>cannot</u> tell
  **A.** what kinds of roles John Wayne played
  **B.** what kind of person *John Wayne* describes
  **C.** whether John Wayne served in the armed forces
  **D.** why John Wayne never served in the armed forces

_____ **2.** This story does <u>not</u> tell
  **A.** the reason for the party
  **B.** how many people came to the party
  **C.** how many people were invited
  **D.** who planned the party

_____ **3.** This influence over people might be called
  **A.** "not seeing the forest for the trees"
  **B.** "finding a diamond in the rough"
  **C.** "seeing beneath the surface"
  **D.** "making the best of a bad thing"

_____ **4.** From this story you can tell that
  **A.** there are no holidays celebrated by all states
  **B.** there is no holiday celebrated by one state alone
  **C.** a national holiday should be called a state holiday
  **D.** all states celebrate the same holidays

_____ **5.** You can tell that the way the insect hears
  **A.** is not its most unusual feature
  **B.** took the scientists a while to understand
  **C.** is through its foot
  **D.** is the same way that people hear

**1.** No one is sure where the word *blimp* comes from. During World War I, the giant balloons were used to catch enemy submarines. As the blimp floated across the sky, the blimp's pilot would see if the blimp had enough gas to keep it up in the air. The pilot would thump the side of the balloon with a thumb. The sound the pilot heard was *blimp*.

**2.** Handwriting can be turned into a form of art called calligraphy. *Calligraphy* means "beautiful writing." Each stroke of the artist's pen or brush makes beautiful ornaments out of the letters. Examples of calligraphy are shown in many art museums.

**3.** There is a bird in India called the tailorbird. It is called this because it sews a nest for its eggs. The bird finds two leaves close together at the end of a branch. It punches holes with its beak along the edges of the leaves. Then it uses natural fibers to sew the leaves into a pocket.

**4.** One architect thinks that buildings in America are starting to look like forts. Many city buildings have blank, windowless walls along the street. These buildings are made for protection against crime. But the architect thinks they make cities less human. This may lead to more crime.

**5.** A leap year is one in which February has an extra, or twenty-ninth, day. This day is needed because each real year lasts a little longer than 365 days. If the extra day weren't added every few years, eventually Thanksgiving would fall in July.

_____ **1.** This story suggests that during World War I
    **A.** there were no submarines in use
    **B.** there was no exact way to measure gas in a blimp
    **C.** blimps had little military use
    **D.** blimps were the only aircraft in use

_____ **2.** Museums display calligraphy because it is
    **A.** a good way of making signs for visitors
    **B.** a work of art
    **C.** helpful in teaching people how to write
    **D.** done with brushes and pens

_____ **3.** You can tell that the tailorbird
    **A.** can be found anywhere in the world
    **B.** was given its name because of the way it flies
    **C.** must be very large
    **D.** has a sharp beak

_____ **4.** From the story you <u>cannot</u> tell
    **A.** what the architect likes about city buildings
    **B.** what many city buildings look like
    **C.** the effect of blank city buildings on people
    **D.** why these buildings are made this way

_____ **5.** From the story you can tell that
    **A.** most years on a calendar have a total of 365 days
    **B.** February has an extra day every twenty-ninth year
    **C.** it isn't possible to figure out the length of a year
    **D.** someday Thanksgiving will come in July

**1.** William James Sidis's father was a Harvard professor who decided to make his son a genius. At 2, Sidis could type in English and in French. At 11 he was the youngest person ever to enter Harvard. After Harvard he retired from public life. He took small jobs and seldom made more than $25 a week.

**2.** Quicksand has its dangers. But it isn't as dangerous as an alkali, or salt, bog. Alkali bogs are dangerous. They are found on hillsides as well as along riverbeds. When people or animals fall into an alkali bog, they sink faster than in quicksand.

**3.** On June 6, 1896, George Harbo and Frank Samuelson set out of New York Harbor. They were in an 18-foot rowboat. They kept rowing until August 1, when they arrived in England. Their only rest was on July 15. That was when a freighter took them aboard and gave them some food.

**4.** Charles Goodyear discovered the process that made rubber into a useful product. His early businesses had failed. He began his rubber experiments while in prison for his debts. Later he sold his ideas about rubber in order to make some money. But he died poor at the age of sixty. He also left his family in debt.

**5.** Scientists know that the world's seas are rising. In the twentieth century, the oceans rose about four inches. But the United States is also sinking slowly. Its sea level rose about one foot over a period of one hundred years.

_____ **1.** From this story you <u>cannot</u> tell
   **A.** which languages Sidis knew
   **B.** what Sidis's father did for a living
   **C.** how Sidis spent his years after graduation
   **D.** why Sidis was not very successful

_____ **2.** You can conclude that quicksand
   **A.** is more dangerous in some ways than an alkali bog
   **B.** usually isn't found on hillsides
   **C.** is nothing to worry about
   **D.** is not similar to an alkali bog

_____ **3.** The two men probably
   **A.** met the freighter during the first half of their trip
   **B.** rowed without stopping to sleep
   **C.** never got out of their boat until reaching England
   **D.** were glad to see the freighter

_____ **4.** You know that Charles Goodyear
   **A.** never worked very hard
   **B.** became rich after inventing the rubber process
   **C.** was cheated out of his fortune
   **D.** never made money from his invention

_____ **5.** From this story you <u>cannot</u> tell
   **A.** who knows that the oceans are rising
   **B.** in which century the oceans rose four inches
   **C.** how much the United States has sunk
   **D.** the cause of the rise in sea level around the world

**1.** Longfellow wrote a poem that made Paul Revere famous for his ride to Concord to warn that the British were coming. Actually, Revere never made it to Concord, nor was he unaccompanied. Two other riders, William Dawes and Dr. Samuel Prescott, went with him. It was Dr. Prescott who warned Concord about the British.

**2.** The United States is full of small, special museums. There is a Sport Fishing Museum in New York, a museum of locks in Connecticut, and the Maple Museum in Vermont. The Lumberman's Museum is located in Maine while the Petrified Creatures Museum is found in New York.

**3.** The parasol ant of South America gets its name from the way it carries a bit of leaf over its head. But native Brazilians call them doctor ants. They use the ants' strong jaws to clamp down on deep cuts and keep them closed. Once the jaws clamp, the Brazilians pinch off the ants' bodies to keep the wound sealed.

**4.** In 1883 a California postal carrier named Jim Stacy found a stray dog, whom he called Dorsey. Dorsey accompanied Stacy on his mail route. But later Stacy got sick. So he tied the mail along with a note to Dorsey's back and sent the dog out alone. Dorsey delivered the mail in this fashion until 1886.

**5.** The odd-looking dodo bird became extinct shortly after it was discovered. In 1598 it was found on an island by a Dutch admiral. The admiral took some birds back with him to Europe. Pictures of the dodo were painted and appeared everywhere. But by 1681 every dodo in the world had died.

_____ **1.** From this story you <u>cannot</u> tell
  **A.** whether the people of Concord were warned
  **B.** how the people of Concord got the warning
  **C.** that Revere never made it to Concord
  **D.** whether or not Longfellow wrote a good poem

_____ **2.** In the Vermont museum, you could probably find
  **A.** a sport fish caught by a lumberman
  **B.** a petrified fish
  **C.** maple syrup buckets
  **D.** a petrified lumberman

_____ **3.** From the story you can tell that
  **A.** parasol ants haven't been named correctly
  **B.** the ants' jaws stay closed after the ants die
  **C.** native Brazilians named the ants "parasol ants"
  **D.** the ants like sunshine

_____ **4.** From this story you can conclude that
  **A.** Stacy was sick for a long time
  **B.** Dorsey would never leave Stacy's side
  **C.** the note told people what to feed Dorsey
  **D.** Dorsey received a medal from the post office

_____ **5.** The story suggests that
  **A.** the discovery of the dodo led to its disappearance
  **B.** the birds were painted for their great beauty
  **C.** the Dutch were good painters
  **D.** the dodo came from Europe originally

**1.** In the seventeenth century, the Inca people of South America had an empire that stretched more than 2,500 miles. They built highways throughout their empire. One of their tunnels extended 750 feet through a mountain cliff. One of their rope suspension bridges is still used today.

**2.** When the Tacoma Narrows Bridge was built in 1940, it was the world's third-largest suspension bridge. Large suspension bridges had been built before. But the builders didn't count on the winds near Tacoma, Washington. Four months after its opening, the bridge was blown down.

**3.** From news reports about Russia, you might think that the Kremlin is a large building in Moscow. Actually, there are many kremlins in Russia. *Kremlin* means "fortress" in Russian. In Moscow the Kremlin is not one building but many buildings inside a walled yard.

**4.** Working at home sounds like fun. You can work in your pajamas. Or you can play the radio as loud as you want. You can even sleep an extra hour in the morning. But making money at home takes drive and dedication. To be successful you must use basic business practices. You must make yourself work rather than play.

**5.** The Egyptian pyramids were built from stones weighing about two and one-half tons each. The structures are forty stories high. The number of stones used in each pyramid could build a wall around France. Yet the Egyptians used no animals. They had no cranes at that time. The wheel wasn't even in use.

_____ **1.** From this story you <u>cannot</u> tell
    **A.** the size of the Inca Empire
    **B.** in what period the Inca lived
    **C.** if the Inca were skilled in engineering
    **D.** why the roads were important to the Inca

_____ **2.** From this story you can conclude that
    **A.** earlier bridges weren't in high-wind areas
    **B.** the Tacoma Narrows Bridge was too large
    **C.** high winds have little effect on suspension bridges
    **D.** the two larger bridges had similar problems

_____ **3.** You can tell that Moscow's Kremlin probably
    **A.** is the only one in Russia
    **B.** is a large building in Russia
    **C.** was originally a fortress
    **D.** is never visited by news reporters

_____ **4.** To be successful you would probably need to
    **A.** stock the refrigerator with plenty of food
    **B.** make a schedule and stick to it
    **C.** plan when to take naps
    **D.** work as little as possible

_____ **5.** You can tell from this story that
    **A.** the Egyptians built a wall around France
    **B.** the work must have been done by many people
    **C.** the pyramids were two and one-half stories high
    **D.** each pyramid weighed about two and one-half tons

**1.** Water going down a drain forms a funnel that spins in one direction. Water always turns in a clockwise direction south of the equator. But north of the equator, water always turns in the opposite direction. The same effect can be seen in the wind funnels of tornadoes. They spin in opposite directions north and south of the equator.

**2.** A caterpillar hangs from a twig using a silk "safety belt" that it has spun. It wiggles slowly out of its old skin without tearing the belt. The caterpillar becomes a pupa. The pupa is very still. But many changes are occurring inside. Finally a butterfly with wings appears. It rests on the twig that once held its safety belt.

**3.** Great Britain may not be the place where golf was first played. The ancient Romans played a similar game. They used a curved stick and a leather ball stuffed with feathers. The Romans occupied Great Britain until A.D. 400.

**4.** The United States Department of Agriculture inspects packages from foreign countries. It makes sure that plant diseases aren't brought into the United States. Dogs are trained to approach airline passengers and sniff for fruits and vegetables. When a dog smells them, it sits down by the passenger carrying them.

**5.** One of the worst volcanic eruptions occurred in 1815. When Mount Tambora blew up, it made a seven-mile hole in its peak. It claimed twelve thousand lives. Later another eighty thousand people died of hunger. The volcanic ash had ruined all the crops.

_____ **1.** From this story you <u>cannot</u> tell
    **A.** how water and wind movements are similar
    **B.** in which direction water spins north of the equator
    **C.** the reason for the differences in direction
    **D.** in which direction a tornado spins in Chile

_____ **2.** Next the butterfly will probably
    **A.** build a pupa
    **B.** find something to eat
    **C.** swim upstream
    **D.** become a caterpillar

_____ **3.** From this story you might conclude that golf
    **A.** began in A.D. 400
    **B.** began in Great Britain and moved to Rome
    **C.** began in Rome and moved to Great Britain
    **D.** is played more in Rome today than in Great Britain

_____ **4.** From the story you <u>cannot</u> tell
    **A.** why the Department of Agriculture inspects packages
    **B.** how dogs help prevent diseases
    **C.** how the dogs alert officials
    **D.** which fruits are not allowed into the country

_____ **5.** You can tell that the greatest damage came
    **A.** from the first explosion of the volcano
    **B.** just before the explosion
    **C.** after the explosion
    **D.** within seven miles of the volcano

**1.** In a radio interview, Albert Einstein was once asked whether he got his great thoughts while in the bathtub, walking, or sitting in his office. Einstein replied, "I don't really know. I've only had one or maybe two."

**2.** Ana carefully filled the bird feeders in her backyard. The many trees that grew on her property were home to various kinds of birds. Ana enjoyed watching the birds and listening to them as they came to eat the seeds she provided for them.

**3.** The special material in our body that makes us who we are is called DNA. Except for identical twins, everybody has different DNA. Since DNA is everywhere in the body, DNA patterns are generally better than fingerprints for identifying people. Police sometimes use DNA patterns to identify suspects.

**4.** Wind does not push sailboats forward. Instead, the sailboats *fall*. The sails on the boat form a curve when the wind passes across them. The curve creates an empty space behind the sail. The boat goes forward by falling into the empty space.

**5.** A comet is like a dirty ball of snow. It is made of frozen gases, frozen water, and dust. As a comet approaches the sun, the icy center gets hot and evaporates. The gases made by the evaporation form the tail of the comet. The dust left behind in the process forms meteor showers.

_____ **1.** From this story you can tell that Einstein
    **A.** thought much like the interviewer
    **B.** enjoyed radio interviews
    **C.** thought too much value was placed on his ideas
    **D.** thought best while walking

_____ **2.** This story does not tell
    **A.** what kind of food Ana gives the birds
    **B.** what kinds of birds come to the bird feeders
    **C.** where the bird feeders are located
    **D.** where the birds lived

_____ **3.** From this story you can tell that
    **A.** some people have no DNA
    **B.** DNA is not found in hair
    **C.** fingerprints are the only way to identify people
    **D.** DNA patterns can help solve crimes

_____ **4.** From this story you cannot tell
    **A.** why the sails on a sailboat form a curve
    **B.** how the sailboat moves forward
    **C.** how an empty space is created
    **D.** how the sails are attached to the boat

_____ **5.** From this story you can tell that
    **A.** comets are made of snow
    **B.** throwing a ball of snow can turn it into a comet
    **C.** the sun helps create the tail of the comet
    **D.** meteor showers are visible with a telescope

**1.** You may think of the contact lens as a fairly new invention. But the first contact lenses were made by a German glassblower in 1887. These contact lenses were ordered by an eye doctor to treat an eye disease. They were made to cover the entire eye.

**2.** Mussels use a powerful glue to attach themselves to rocks underwater. Now scientists have found a way to make the glue in the laboratory. The glue isn't affected by water or salt. It can be used to glue fillings into teeth. The glue can even be used to join badly broken bones.

**3.** The Apollo space program sent men to the moon. These astronauts returned to Earth with nearly 840 pounds of moon rocks. Most of them are now in Houston, Texas. People have been looking closely at the rocks. So far, the rocks have not shown where the moon came from. But scientists continue to borrow pieces to study.

**4.** The two world wars were not the wars that took the greatest number of American lives. The most costly war in American lives was the Civil War. At least 524,000 soldiers died in that conflict. That number is one-fifth greater than the number of American soldiers who died in World War II.

**5.** People sleepwalk only during very deep sleep. If you awaken a sleepwalker, he or she will not remember any dreams. People dream during a lighter sleep. The dreamer's closed eyes may move back and forth rapidly. If you see a sleeping person's eyes move and you awaken the person, the person may be able to remember vivid dreams.

◯

_____ **1.** From this story you <u>cannot</u> tell
    **A.** what the first contact lenses were for
    **B.** where the person who made the first pair was from
    **C.** whether the first contact lenses were successful
    **D.** how long contact lenses have been in existence

_____ **2.** From this story you can tell that
    **A.** mussels do not have bones or teeth
    **B.** the laboratory glue is very expensive
    **C.** water and salt reduce the strength of most glues
    **D.** mussels move from one place to another

_____ **3.** From the Apollo missions, scientists
    **A.** learned the origin of Earth
    **B.** may learn the origin of the moon
    **C.** took the rocks to Washington, D.C.
    **D.** refused to let other people see the rocks

_____ **4.** From this story you might conclude that
    **A.** the Civil War lasted one year
    **B.** World War II ranks second in lives lost
    **C.** Americans fought only in Vietnam
    **D.** the American Revolution cost many lives

_____ **5.** You can tell that
    **A.** sleepwalkers probably don't dream
    **B.** the best sleep is very deep
    **C.** vivid dreams help people sleep
    **D.** people dream during a deep sleep

**1.** Men and women have different habits. When men sip drinks, they usually look into the cup. Women usually look above the rim. Men often examine their nails with their palms facing toward them and their fingers curled. But women view their nails by turning their palms away and holding their fingers straight up.

**2.** Nations fight wars for many reasons. In the 1880s a war between the United States and Great Britain almost started because of a pig. The trouble took place on an island off the coast of Washington state. An American killed a pig owned by a British man. Tempers flared, and troops were sent to the island. The dispute, known as the Pig War, was soon settled without any fighting.

**3.** Harvey Gartley of Michigan did not really want to become a boxer. Maybe that's why he lost a fight without ever being hit. The boy was in a Golden Gloves match. As his opponent swung and jabbed, Gartley danced just out of reach. But he danced too much and soon fell from exhaustion. The match was over in 47 seconds. Gartley lost, but his parents were glad that he hadn't been hurt.

**4.** Mongooses are small Asian mammals that kill poisonous snakes and rats. In the 1890s sugar planters in Hawaii imported mongooses to control the rats there. But the planters made a big mistake. They learned too late that mongooses roam by day, while rats roam by night. Now mongooses are a pest problem in Hawaii.

**5.** Tom Evans was on a field trip in Big Bend National Park in Texas. He and his college classmates had come from Chicago to hunt for fossils. As he was searching, Evans spotted something sticking out of a dirt mound. It turned out to be a major discovery. Evans had found the complete skull of a dinosaur. The four-foot-long skull came from a chasmosaurus, which resembled a rhinoceros. The skull had been buried for about eighty million years.

_____ **1.** From this story you <u>cannot</u> tell
    **A.** how men examine their fingernails
    **B.** why men and women do things differently
    **C.** how men sip drinks
    **D.** how women view their nails

_____ **2.** The story suggests that
    **A.** many soldiers were injured in the war
    **B.** the war was fought in Europe
    **C.** the pig was cooked when the war ended
    **D.** some arguments can get out of hand

_____ **3.** You can conclude that Gartley
    **A.** didn't have much boxing talent
    **B.** won the fight
    **C.** fell on his opponent
    **D.** made his parents angry

_____ **4.** From this story you can tell that
    **A.** mongooses like to eat sugarcane
    **B.** rats are poisonous
    **C.** mongooses like to hula dance at night
    **D.** the sugar planters made their problems worse

_____ **5.** From the story you <u>cannot</u> tell
    **A.** what Evans found at Big Bend
    **B.** where Evans made his discovery
    **C.** what grade Evans made for his field trip
    **D.** what kind of dinosaur the skull belonged to

# Writing

Read each paragraph. Think about a conclusion you can draw. Write your conclusion in a complete sentence.

**1.** Cesar Gutierrez wasn't the greatest baseball player. He played in only 223 big league games. But on June 21, 1970, he performed a great batting feat for the Detroit Tigers. In a game that went 12 innings, Cesar made 7 hits in a row. On that day the shortstop from Coro, Venezuela, was perfect!

What conclusion can you draw from this paragraph?

_____

_____

**2.** Ashton considers himself a student of the game of chess. He spends his spare time in games with others. He often plays games at home with his friends. Sometimes he plays games on the computer with people who live far away. He hopes to be a champion someday.

What conclusion can you draw from this paragraph?

_____

_____

**3.** Pearl Mae Bailey was born in Virginia in 1918. She became a movie and television star. She won a Tony Award for her starring role in the African American version of the musical *Hello Dolly*. In honor of her outstanding career and work with the United Nations, she was awarded the Presidential Medal of Freedom.

What conclusion can you draw from this paragraph?

_____

_____

**To check your answers, turn to page 60.**

Read the paragraph below. What conclusions can you draw? Use the clues in the paragraph to answer the questions in complete sentences.

> Long before people kept written records, they used spoken words to pass along their customs and history. In Africa young people who show some skill in telling stories are still urged to practice it. In Western Africa people who tell tales from history are known as *griots*. These oral artists often use music with their tales. Through their stories, they entertain people. And they give their people a clear sense of their past. In return, the people give the griots much love and respect.

**1.** Is the spoken word still used to preserve history in Africa? How do you know?

_____

_____

**2.** Do Africans think that only old people should practice story-telling? How do you know?

_____

_____

**3.** Do griots always tell their tales the same way? How do you know?

_____

_____

**4.** Do Africans like the griots? How do you know?

_____

_____

**To check your answers, turn to page 60.**

Conclusion • Level F

# Check Yourself

**Using What You Know, Page 3**

at a job interview, at a car wash, at a traffic light, on a mountain

**Practice Drawing Conclusions, Page 4**

2. B

**To check your answers to pages 6–29, see page 61.**

**Writing, Page 30**

Possible answers include:

1. You can't play polo if you can't ride a horse.
2. Phillis Wheatley was good with languages.
3. Alonso's weather station isn't finished yet.

**Writing, Page 31**

Possible answers include:

1. Juneteenth is not a holiday in all states. It is celebrated only by people in Texas and in some other states.
2. There was slavery in Texas. Union troops ended slavery there.
3. Texans did not know the Civil War had ended. The Union troops told them.
4. Californians did not coin the word *Juneteenth*. People in Texas created this word.

**To check your answers to pages 32–57, see page 62.**

**Writing, Page 58**

Possible answers include:

1. Cesar Gutierrez wasn't born in the United States.
2. Ashton knows how to use a computer to play chess.
3. Pearl Bailey was an actress.

**Writing, Page 59**

Possible answers include:

1. The spoken word is still used to preserve history in Africa. Griots tell stories about the past.
2. Africans do not think that only old people should practice story-telling. They urge some young people to practice it.
3. Griots do not always tell the tales the same way. They often use music but not always.
4. Africans like the griots. They love and respect them.

# Check Yourself

| Unit 1 pp. 6–7 | Unit 2 pp. 8–9 | Unit 3 pp. 10–11 | Unit 4 pp. 12–13 | Unit 5 pp. 14–15 | Unit 6 pp. 16–17 | Unit 7 pp. 18–19 | Unit 8 pp. 20–21 | Unit 9 pp. 22–23 | Unit 10 pp. 24–25 | Unit 11 pp. 26–27 | Unit 12 pp. 28–29 |
|---|---|---|---|---|---|---|---|---|---|---|---|
| 1. C | 1. D | 1. D | 1. B | 1. C | 1. B | 1. D | 1. C | 1. A | 1. D | 1. A | 1. C |
| 2. D | 2. D | 2. C | 2. C | 2. C | 2. A | 2. C | 2. B | 2. A | 2. C | 2. D | 2. A |
| 3. B | 3. A | 3. B | 3. D | 3. A | 3. B | 3. B | 3. D | 3. C | 3. A | 3. B | 3. B |
| 4. A | 4. D | 4. A | 4. A | 4. C | 4. C | 4. D | 4. C | 4. D | 4. B | 4. C | 4. D |
| 5. C | 5. A | 5. D | 5. A | 5. D | 5. C | 5. B | 5. A | 5. A | 5. B | 5. C | 5. B |

| Unit 13 pp. 32–33 | Unit 14 pp. 34–35 | Unit 15 pp. 36–37 | Unit 16 pp. 38–39 | Unit 17 pp. 40–41 | Unit 18 pp. 42–43 | Unit 19 pp. 44–45 | Unit 20 pp. 46–47 | Unit 21 pp. 48–49 | Unit 22 pp. 50–51 | Unit 23 pp. 52–53 | Unit 24 pp. 54–55 | Unit 25 pp. 56–57 |
|---|---|---|---|---|---|---|---|---|---|---|---|---|
| 1. D | 1. D | 1. C | 1. D | 1. D | 1. B | 1. D | 1. D | 1. D | 1. C | 1. C | 1. C | 1. B |
| 2. B | 2. C | 2. A | 2. A | 2. B | 2. B | 2. B | 2. C | 2. A | 2. B | 2. B | 2. C | 2. D |
| 3. A | 3. C | 3. C | 3. C | 3. C | 3. D | 3. D | 3. B | 3. C | 3. C | 3. D | 3. B | 3. A |
| 4. C | 4. A | 4. D | 4. B | 4. C | 4. A | 4. D | 4. A | 4. B | 4. D | 4. D | 4. B | 4. D |
| 5. A | 5. B | 5. D | 5. D | 5. B | 5. A | 5. D | 5. A | 5. B | 5. C | 5. C | 5. A | 5. C |